'Haud Yer Wheesht!'
Your Scottish Granny's Favourite Sayings

Allan Morrison

ILLUSTRATED BY

NEIL WILSON PUBLISHING, GLASGOW, SCOTLAND

Published by Neil Wilson Publishing Ltd
303a The Pentagon Centre
36 Washington Street,
GLASGOW
G3 8AZ

Tel: 0141-221-1117
Fax: 0141-221-5363
E-mail: nwp@cqm.co.uk
http://www.nwp.co.uk/

A catalogue record for this book is available
from the British Library.

ISBN 1-897784-60-0

Dedicated to grannies everywhere

Designed by Mark Blackadder

Typeset in Bodoni by The Write Stuff
E-mail: wilson_i@cqm.co.uk

Printed by the Cromwell Press

CONTENTS

Introduction   v
Grannies on …
      1   Business   7
      2   Communication   9
      3   Death   12
      4   Decisions   14
      5   Drink   15
      6   Evil   16
      7   Family Life   18
      8   Food   23
      9   Friendship   25
     10   The Future   27
     11   God   28
     12   Happiness   29
     13   Health   33
     14   Helping Others   37
     15   Honesty   38
     16   Human Behaviour   40
     17   Improving Yourself   47
     18   Life's Experiences   51
     19   Love   54
     20   Marriage   56
     21   Memories   57
     22   Money   58
     23   Observations on Life   61
     24   Old Folks   67
     25   Patience   69
     26   Possessions   70
     27   Practical Actions   72
     28   Reputations   77
     29   Respect   79
     30   Shrewdness   80
     31   Taking Positive Measures   86
     32   Time   92
     33   Weather   93
     34   Work   95
Glossary   96

INTRODUCTION

Life is a hazardous business, is it not? To negotiate it successfully, we each need at least a small share of wise caution, or prudence if you like. For a happy passage we also need some wit and imagination too. And, for the life we truly want, a portion of hard-headedness is of no small use, a stubborn streak being just the thing for the individual.

Scotland is a hospitable, accessible and exciting land which lies to the North of Hadrian's Wall. Down through the ages, the Scots have been providers of useful and influential historic breakthroughs. As a nation of inventors (penicillin, television, chloroform, the steam engine, logarithms, etc to name a few) we have given the world major practical creations. Now we offer the faculty of common sense from our family historians — our Scottish grandmothers.

Centuries of meditative reasoning, contemplative wanderings and the hard slog that is French café life have come up with little better than '... all I know is that I do not know'. Grannies do better than this. My granny didn't say, 'I think, therefore I am'. That sort of thing is not suitably shrewd, nor is it overly entertaining.

Grandmothers are endowed with level-headed practicality. Lots of grannies are! Certainly,

Scottish ones are a special breed. They have had wisdom passed down to them either directly or through the 'second sight' (that curious ability to see a little way into the future). This is a compilation of over 500 observations on life obtained from numerous mature, astute and worldly-wise elderly ladies of distinction. Some of the sayings are ancient — some contemporary. In each case, the Scottish vernacular is cited first and a translation follows for those of you not familiar with the Scots tongue (and there's a handy glossary at the back of the book to help you along).

This book is, in part, my way of adding to or maintaining the Scots language — something I've never really done before. It is the gift of maturity to those who need it, common sense to those who lack it and worldly wisdom to all. Hopefully, it will stimulate some folks and challenge others. Follow granny's sayings and have a long and happy life … and remember, if you are ever in doubt about what to say, it is probably best to say nothing — or as granny used to put it, 'Haud yer wheesht!'

1 BUSINESS

Oot on the branch, the fruit is gey ripe.
The most successful ventures entail the greatest risks.

If ye dinna see the bottom, dinna wade.
Don't go into a venture if you can't see your way through
with it.

The cow may want her tail yet.
You may want a favour in the future from me, though
you're not giving me one right now!

First offer's ne'er accepted.
People who advertise 'first reasonable offer accepted',
never accept it.

Trade wi' honest men and ye talk to few.
Honest businessmen are few and far between.

Don't test the depth of the burn wi' both feet.
Don't commit everything to one venture.

The stars shine brightest when the moon is on the wane.
When large concerns falter, opportunities arise to further your own business.

A freen at court is worth a penny in the purse.
Maintaining good contacts is always worthwhile.

He's a fool that asks ower muckle and a bigger fool that gives it.
A fool will ask for too much, but a bigger fool will agree to give him it.

2 COMMUNICATION

A nod's as guid as a wink tae a blind horse.
Always ensure you make your meaning clear.

Nae post then send a post.
When you don't receive a letter — send a letter.

Kindly words are best for the mooth.
Say gentle words only — you may have to eat them later.

Haud yer wheesht!
Be quiet!

Birds and blethers fly.
Rumours travel as quickly as birds.

A wee bit disagreement keeps the talk lang.
Too much agreement kills a conversation.

Haud on a wee minent.
Slow down and take your time.

Nicht is the mither o' thoughts.
Many profound thoughts come at night.

Think twice on a' thing
Don't make decisions hastily. Second thoughts are usually
better than the first ones.

E'en guid sermons cause a snore.
Even the best communicators have their faults.

Hae a guid whittle at yer belt.
It pays to have a ready answer.

Blethers say nought.
People who say too much say nothing.

Some folks' minds are like the wind in a winter's nicht.
Some people's contributions are valueless.

Talkin' discloses a' tae the folk in the street.
Never say too much in public!

Dinna clothe your language in ragged attire.
Don't spoil what you say by using bad language.

A tongue's a fearsome tool.
What you say can be a powerful asset

Nae words, nae quarrel.
If you stay silent, no one can argue with you.

3 DEATH

Time and thinking tame the strongest grief.
Time and contemplation are the greatest healers of grief.

Hae life right to the end.
Live as though tomorrow were your last.

It's no the ramblin' cart that fa's first ower the brae.
It's not always the person you expect who dies first.

Folk may die, but the toon clock will chime again.
People die but life goes on.

Relations are a wilful lot.
Relatives can be stubborn over wills.

Toilin's the hard bit — dyin's easy.
Dying is easy — it's living that's hard.

Thon doctors canny keep you goin' forever.
Doctors only postpone death.

Death's the cost o' living.
Death is the payment we make for living.

**Dinna look for death — it'll come and find you
sure enough.**
Death is inevitable.

Heaven dims wi' good health.
Thoughts of one's mortality recede when in good health.

At death's door oor life begins.
Death is not the way out — it is the way in.

Even gentry hae but a short time here.
Even landowners live on borrowed property.

He's got the look o' wet cley aboot him.
He looks as though he is dying.

4 DECISIONS

Double check your measure afore you cut.
Consider well before you make final decisions.

Here's yer meat — tak it or leave it.
You've two choices in many situations.

Twa' wrongs can dim the morrow.
Two wrongs may not make a right but they do make a
dangerous precedent.

Crooked hooses cam fae committees.
It is better to make your own decisions.

Ye canna sell the cow and sup the milk too.
You cannot have it both ways.

It's as plain as the nose on yer face!
The solution is surely clear!

Say 'no' and ye'll no go far wrang.
Sometimes, saying 'no' is a positive thing to do.

**Naething to be done in haste but grippin' o'
fleas.**
Never act hastily — unless you're trying to kill flies.

5 DRINK

A red nose maks a ragged back.
If you drink to excess, you may have no money for
necessities.

Watch them waur to drink than to corn.
Be wary of those who spend their money on drink, rather
than food.

Drink little, that ye may drink lang.
Too much alcohol shortens the lifespan.

A dram brings truth unco close.
Beware, whisky brings out the truth.

6 EVIL

Bad yins smile too.
There is good and bad in everyone.

'Nae conscience' is given a wide berth.
Beware of people with no conscience or feelings.

The deil's bairns hae aye their daddy's luck.
Some rogues seem to have the luck of the devil.

He that ill does, never guid weens.
There is nothing good to be gained from badness.

An idle brain is the deil's smiddy.
Do nothing and the devil will give you a task.

A scabbit sheep will smit a hail herself.
One evil person can infect the whole.

The wan wi' the ladder's as bad as the thief.
Don't associate with rogues.

7 Family Life

Aye pat the richt end o' the wean.
Child rearing is merely knowing which end of your child to pat.

A guid hame has guid children.
A loving family produces well-balanced children.

Weans hae nae politics.
Be childlike and you'll see the world without prejudice.

Weans wi' big ears take it a' in.
Watch how you speak in front of children.

A balanced opinion's due a wean.
Compliment children when they do well; reassure them when they fail.

Better plays the fou' wame than the new coat.
It is better to feed your children well than to clothe them
well.

Gang carefu' in spilin' the weans.
Sometimes doing more for your child means doing less.

A' mithers go to work.
All mothers are working mothers.

Weans may not listen, but they copy you.
Even though you think children are not listening — they
still copy you.

**Observe the bairns through your neighbours'
eyes.**
Try and see your children as they are seen by others.

**Between three and thirteen, thran the woodie
when it's green.**
It is best to train children early in life.

It's just ma' weans that's perfect!
Only other folks children are spoiled!

Bairns maun creep 'ere they gang.
Those who don't succeed at first may well do better later.

East or west, hame is best.
There's no place like home.

Act like a guest in yer ain hoose.
Folk should behave in their own homes as though they
were guests.

A cat's a tiger in his ain hoose.
In your own home, you're boss.

Young folk know a' thing.
Young folk think they know it all.

Fresh eyes at hame see a' thing.
Visitors see more in a minute than hosts in a lifetime.

We can shape our bairns' wylie-coat, but canna shape their weird.
You might determine what your child wears — but not its future.

Every bird thinks its ain nest's best.
We all like familiar surroundings.

Burnt bairns dread the fire.
We all learn from life's sore experiences.

A rich man has mair cousins than his father had kin.
A rich person attracts 'family'.

Dinna be a hoose deil and a causey saint.
Don't be a devil at home and a saint elsewhere.

As the auld cock craws, the young cock learns.
The young learn from the actions of their elders.

Today's troubles affect tomorrow's bairns.
We create problems today which affect our children when
they grow up.

If ye break yer legs, don't come running to me!
If you don't do as I tell you, don't come to me for help!

8 Food

Hunger is the best kitchen.
Food tastes better when you're hungry.

As the sow fills, the draff sours.
The more you eat, the less you relish your food.

Hunger wid break through stane wa's.
Hunger can drive people to desperation.

Suppin' loud's nae company.
Don't slurp when supping soup.

Better a sma' fish than an empty dish.
Better to have something to eat than nothing at all.

An eating horse ne'er foundered.
It is a healthy sign when people eat well.

Some folks cannae see green cheese but their e'en reels.
Some folk love food regardless of its condition.

Stoke up wi' the purridge.
Without a hearty start to the day, you'll soon tire.

Maist accidents are served up!
Most accidents happen in the kitchen.

9 FRIENDSHIP

It's nae loss, what a freen gets.
You don't really lose something if your friend gets it.

Hae freens and hae life.
Good friends result in a full life..

Try and mak freens o' the unlikely.
Don't be put off by appearances.

Comfort comes in auld clothes.
Familiar friends are the best to comfort you.

Guid company on a journey is worth a coach.
Good company improves any journey.

Mony freens gae a happy life.
Friendship brings happiness.

Want a freen — be a freen.
Treat others as you would expect them to treat you.

Old boots and freens are a comfort.
Friends are like old boots: comforting, dependable, durable and warm.

A dug or cat can be a freen.
When you're lonely, don't forget that your pets are also your friends.

Rich folks wi' nae money test their freens.
Friendship is not dependent on wealth; adversity will
prove true friendship.

When we want, freens are scant.
In times of need, our friends can be few.

**Stay nae langer in a freen's hoose than you're
welcome.**
Never overstay a welcome.

10 The Future

Only yersel' can unwrap yer future.
You are in charge of your own destiny.

Live noo — no back.
Live for today. Never dwell on the past.

Look afront tae where you'll live.
Look only to the future (because that's where you'll spend
the rest of your days).

Do a'thing as in the last day.
Undertake every action as though it were your last.

What's for ye will no' go by ye.
What is meant for you in life, you will receive.

11 GOD

If God listens to a' mens' prayers, he must be scunnered.
If God dealt with every request, he would feel sickened.

A minister's gey obvious but cunnin'!
You can always recognise a minister, but you can't preach to him.

Nae faith's gey dry.
Without faith, life is meaningless.

God sends us claith according to our cauld.
The Lord provides according to our needs.

He who serves God is the truly wise man.
Having a belief gives life purpose and makes folks wise.

12 HAPPINESS

A happy wean is a happy wean.
If you believe you are happy — you are.

Rainbows come out o' rain's drips.
To know joy you must know sorrow.

A contented mind beats bein' the king.
It is better to be content than be in a high position.

A guid laugh shows yer a' aboot.
Laughter is the sound of feeling good all over.

Generous folks are happy yins.
Helpful people are happy people.

Picnic spots are always better further on.
Be content with your lot.

Contentment is gey rich.
If you are happy, then you are rich.

A body should be in the fashion and smile.
Smile — you don't need a special size for it to fit.

Greatest wealth is contentment wi' little.
Accepting what you've got makes you wealthy.

Peace o' mind's not in the shops.
You cannot buy peace of mind.

Happiness within gaes a glow.
Inner peace is the ultimate joy.

Laughin' folk are a' rich.
You're never poor if you can laugh.

He's no the happiest man that has the maist gear.
Possessions won't bring you happiness.

Folks happy at home dinna go far to war.
Contented people do not go out of their way to make trouble.

Ye could gang faur an' fare waur.
You could travel a lot further and do worse than your present situation.

A shinin' face comes fae light.
Goodness can make you more appealing.

Dinna be wan who could moan for Scotland.
Don't tell everyone about your woes; keep your problems
to yourself.

**Some folks are all away to the wan side like
Gourock.**
A balanced outlook on life is best.

Richt wrangs nae man.
Goodness has no bad effects on anyone.

Dinna trouble trouble till trouble troubles you.
Don't go looking for trouble.

13 HEALTH

Pit a fastin' spittle on yer pimples.
Put saliva on your spots before you eat breakfast. (An old
Scottish remedy for warts and pimples!)

Better health than wealth.
Health is more important than wealth.

A sair back maks ye think.
Pain can make us consider our life.

Only clean oot yer ear wi' yer elbow.
Don't damage your own health.

**Clean yer wallies thrice and they stay in twice as
lang.**
Clean your teeth three times a day; they'll live to bite
another day!

Dinna fash yersel.
Don't worry.

Being sorry for yersel's nae medicine.
Self pity won't cure your ills.

Ane hour in the morn is worth twa at nicht.
You achieve more when you're fresh and energetic.

Stay young wi' an open mind.
Be willing to accept change.

**Lang may yer lum reek — an' may he huv the
coal tae fill it.**
May you live long and well.

'This won't hurt', aye did!
When they say 'This won't hurt' — watch out!

**He what eats but ane dish seldom needs the
doctor.**
Don't overeat!

A' folks hae the same illnesses.
You're not unique!

A guid wife and health is a man's best wealth.
Health and a good partner are life's real wealth.

Wi' guid porridge yer a' richt for life.
With proper care, your body will last a lifetime!

Ye're buttoned up the back like Achmahoy's dug.
You're so thin, your spine sticks out of your back.

Nae pain, big blessin'.
A body free from pain is a great blessing

Up and doon the same day gives health.
Going to bed on the same day you got up is healthy.

Kame sindle, kame sair.
If you don't comb your hair, it'll be sore when you do.

She's a skinny malinky lang legs.
She's very tall and slim.

**Watch you don't get 'Brechan Mareushan
Tartan'.**
If you sit in front of the fire, your legs will go red and
blotchy.

A guid walk cures the mind.
Exercise cures melancholy.

Suppers kill mair than doctors cure.
Overeating shortens life.

Muckle coo meat; mony maladies.
Too much beef in your diet causes illness.

14 HELPING OTHERS

Gae attention to those who attend you.
Be good to those who are good to you.

A helpin' haun helps twa.
Helping another helps improve yourself too.

Pleasure comes from doin' good.
The gain in doing something good is to have done it.

Tell anither, tell yersel'.
Instruct another and learn twice yourself.

Sufferin' for a freen doubleth freenship.
Putting yourself out for a friend strengthens the
relationship.

Gae aye person yer charity.
Charity may begin at home but it should not end there.

Gae it oot and get it back.
What we give, we have.

Giving to charity increaseth a man's store.
Give to charity and you will grow in stature.

Spend, and God will send; spare, and be bare.
Be generous in your giving and your life.

15 HONESTY

Lock yer door and keep yer neighbour honest.
Don't put temptation in the way of your neighbour.

You promised me these would be fine —

Guid shortbread an' promises aye crumble.
Promises are as fragile as shortbread.

Some thieves are honest men wi' temptation.
Opportunity makes thieves of honest men.

The nod o' an honest man is enough.
Honest men don't need contracts.

Tell the truth an' shame the deil.
Always tell the truth.

Honest men dinna carry salmon under their coat.

There is no need to hide something gained with honest toil.

An honest face is a guid yin.

Sincerity is more valuable than good appearances.

16 HUMAN BEHAVIOUR

Baith sexes moan.
Nobody's perfect.

He that winna be counselled, canna be helped.
If you ignore advice, you only have yourself to blame.

There's naething got by delay, but dirt and lang nails.
Don't procrastinate.

A wumman buys, a man supplies.
Women look for the bargains, the men pay for them.

Yin brave beats a' feart.
One courageous person is better than any number of cowards.

Eat peas wi' a prince and cherries wi' a chapman.
Treat all men equally.

Anger's mair hurtful than the wrang that's caused it.
Anger is always more damaging than its cause.

Nae whip cuts sae sharp as the lash o' conscience.
There's nothing worse than a guilty conscience.

Bad temper maks a problem worse.
Losing your temper won't cure anything.

Even some Sassenachs are guid!
There are good people everywhere.

Falsehood maks ye false.
Lying is self-betrayal.

Ne'er let your gear gang you.
Don't just pride yourself in material things.

If the de'il finds an idle man, he sets him to work.
If you're not busy you may end up doing the wrong things.

Eagles flee alane, but sheep herd the gither.
Individualists will always stand out from the crowd.

Pointin' means wan finger oot and three to yersel.
Sometimes we are more at fault than those we find fault with.

Guilty consciences dinna need the polis.
A guilty conscience doesn't need a prosecutor.

Jealous judges are nae fair.
Jealousy can cloud your judgement.

Anger begins wi' folly an ends wi' repentance.
Anger is the product of foolishness and is always regretted.

The deil's aye guid tae his ain kin.
Some rogues always seem to prosper.

Hittin' yer dug wi' a big stick is easy.
You will always find a reason to justify any action.

God gave folks wan face but a' use anither.
Few people reveal their true selves.

Ower helpin' maks naebody aware o' the burden.
If you're carrying somebody they do not appreciate the difficulties of the journey.

He that will be angry for onything, will be angry for naething.
Bad tempered folk are bad tempered about anything.

Anger maks a rich man hated and a poor man scorned.
Anger wins no friends whether you're rich or poor.

Gae a beggar a bed and he'll pay ye wi' a louse.
Being kind to some folks can rebound on you.

Ye wad marry a midden for the muck.
Some people are so mean they would wed a dustbin for its contents!

A vaunter and a liar are muckle aboot a' thing.
People who exaggerate or lie are very similar.

A greedy e'e ne'er gat a fou wame
Greedy folk are never satisfied.

Telling it true, pits ain in a stew.
Telling the truth confuses your enemies.

Ye do whit yer thinking.
The actions of men betray their inner thoughts.

Praise the deaf an' see a miracle.
Sometimes when we compliment a deaf person, they hear you perfectly.

A wolf may lose his teeth but ne'er his nature.
Watch out! Some people never change.

Langest at the fireside, soonest finds cauld.
Spoiled people find it difficult to cope with life's downturns.

A dog winna yowl if ye strike him wi' a bane.
Give a person what they want and they'll not complain.

Courtesy is cumbersome to them that ken it no.
Mannerless people find manners a burden.

Dinna pour water on a drowned moose.
Don't undertake unnecessary actions.

Yon thinks all her eggs hae twa yolks.
Some people always think themselves superior.

There's nowt sae queer as folk.
There is nothing as unpredictable as people in this life.

Envy and self slow folks doon.
Jealousy and selfishness are vices to be avoided.

I'll give you laldie!
I'll give you more than just a telling off!

Shy and timid folk are no fully happy.
Happiness is not a friend of the shy and timid.

Yon has mair faces than the toon clock.
He is not to be trusted.

17 IMPROVING YOURSELF

Being busy improves yer mind.
Work expands the mind.

Wink at sma' faults. Ye hae great anes yoursel.
Don't criticise people. We've all got our faults.

The first step to virtue is to love it in anither.
Appreciate virtue in others and gain it yourself.

Bad mistakes provide a man wi' quick experience.
Experience comes quickly when we learn from our mistakes.

Ower rest causes nae movement.
Too much resting causes stagnation.

Better be the head o' the commons than the tail o' the gentry.
Better to be top of your league than bottom of a higher one.

Gaelic pits new soul intae ye.
Understanding Gaelic enlightens the mind.

Only measure yer shadow wi' a high sun.
Don't be bigheaded.

Adversity breeds character intae yin.
Character is developed in tough situations.

Mockin's catchin'!
If you mock someone, you mock yourself.

A stumble helps ye richt yer fall.
Stumbling can sometimes prevent a fall.

Slow fires mak sweet meat.
Take your time to achieve perfection.

Losing the heid and madness are brithers.
There's a fine line between anger and madness.

Following a fool is foolish.
Copy only those worth copying.

Nae rain and just sun maks a' deed.
Variety is the spice of life.

A'body should have a guid conceit o' themselves.
Pride and confidence are essential to self-improvement.

Auld sparrows are ill to tame.
It's difficult to change the ways of a mature person.

Guid claes and keys let ye in.
Dressing well can open doors for you — just as a key can.

'Bad' is never 'even worse'.
Sometimes it is better to stay the way you are.

Experience teaches fools and fools willna learn nae ither way.
Foolish people only learn through bitter experience.

If a' men stick tae their talent the coos wid be well milked.
If all men did what they were good at the world would be a better place.

Readin's fur improvin'.
Reading betters you..

Do weel and dread nae shame.
If you do your best you have nothing to be ashamed of.

Imagination maks the mind big.
Imagination is the oxygen of our minds.

Clean minds bring nae shame.
A healthy mind has nothing to be ashamed of.

Worry blunts yer blade.
Worrying takes the edge off your performance.

A wise man gets learnin' frae them that hae nane to themselves.
You can learn something from everybody in this world.

Be what you seem; and seem what you are.
Be the way you project yourself.

Adversity testeth the maun.
Adversity is the true test of character.

Better master ane than fight wi' ten.
Better to be good at one thing than struggle with a lot.

A bad wound may heal, but a bad name will kill.
A bad reputation will never go away.

18 LIFE'S EXPERIENCES

Speak o' the deil and he'll appear.
Talk about someone and they'll surely appear.

Read old books fae folks long awa'.
Respect the teachings of wise folk long since passed on.

Dinna remove ancient landmarks fae oor fathers.
Keep the standards established by past generations.

A wee keek back keeps ye on the right path.
Let life's experiences guide you forward.

Dae ye think I come up the Clyde on a bike?
Do you think I'm an idiot?

Fallin' weans are sorry but wiser.
By making mistakes, we can only become wiser.

Some compliments cost awfy dear.
Watch out — some folk pay dearly for compliments.

Slow doon on lost paths.
Don't run if you don't know where you are going.

Jokin's fine tae owercome nae sense.
Humour is useful when common sense is in short supply.

Calm waters gae nae skill tae tars.
Easy tasks won't enhance your skills.

Sodgers wi' big guns beat sodgers wi' pretty dresses.
Being practical is more important than being presentable.

Failing at least means yer playin'.
Even if you don't succeed, it's important to have tried.

Wee stones, not big hills, trip the unwary.
It's sometimes the less obvious problems that can trip you up.

When it gets really dark, you can see stars.
Even the most difficult situations have benefits.

Frights cause quick learning.
Better than good advice is a good scare!

Skilled tars need nae luck wi' the wind.
Experienced folk will overcome any situation.

Silent dugs also bite.
Assume nothing in this life.

Wrinkles are painted wi' a brush o' experience.
Age represents experience.

It's not darkness that puts oot the candle.
In any situation, consider all the factors.

19 LOVE

Look after your loving always or it gangs wrang.
Be attentive to those who love you or their love may fade.

Love is as warm amang cottars as courtiers.
Love is special regardless of your position in life.

Love owercomes the reasons o' mind.
The heart always rules the head.

Love runs oot suspicion's gate.
Suspicion and love are incompatible.

True love's fearless.
Love conquers all.

Love's wan e'e and ower deef.
Love is almost blind and a bit deaf.

Gae yer neighbours aw chances.
Try and love your neighbours.

Lovers fool awfy easy.
Love impairs your judgment.

When petticoats woo, breeks may come speed.
When the fair sex indicate interest, the males come
running.

A bonny wife and a big back door aften maks a man poor.

People with pretty partners should be on guard!

Mak sure yer ain are telt ye love them.

Always tell your loved ones that you do love them.

Love and the cold catch on.

Love is as infectious as the common cold.

20 MARRIAGE

He wha's poor when he marries shall be rich when he's buried.
Marriage improves your lot in life.

Never marry a widow, unless her first husband was hanged.
The good first husband of a widow is a difficult act to follow.

Better marry ower the midden that ower the muir.
It is better to marry in your own circle of people.

Mony ane for land, taks a fool by the haun.
Some people marry for one reason only — money.

Guid husbands fix the bairn — ithers only wake you.
Poor husbands won't attend to a baby in the middle of the night!

You and him should get merrit — nae use spilin' twa hooses!
Some folks should marry each other rather than spoil other marriages.

Trust in the Lord but keep yer e'en on yer man.
Be faithful to God, but watch your partner below!

21 MEMORIES

Nicht thochts bring happiness roon again.
Memories are a second opportunity for happiness.

When sorrow sleeps, wake it not.
Don't keep thinking of past sorrows.

Sow guid memory for the comin' seasons.
Memory is a good garden; it can bloom in all seasons of
the year.

Folks remember well the smell o' growin' up
The smell of childhood can be a sweet remembrance.

Aw folk have convenient memories.
All people tend to remember only what they want to.

Yer mind forgives but disnae forget.
Indiscretion cannot be forgotten, but can be forgiven.

22 Money

If ye had a'thing, whar wad ye keep it?
You can't have everything in this world.

Dae ye need it? Then it micht be a bargain.
A bargain is only a bargain if you need it.

Thanks is guid pey.
The best pay is to receive thanks.

Cut yer coat accordin' tae yer pattern.
Spend only what you can afford.

Nae problem is real money.
The greatest of all riches is peace of mind.

If yer ain siller buys it, it'll be polished.
Pay for an item yourself and you'll take more care of it.

Wi' an empty haun nae man can hawks lure.
You get nothing for nothing in this world.

Keep slim within yer jacket's seam.
Don't live beyond your means.

Lay yer wame to your winning.
Don't spend more than you earn.

Mak yer siller then haud on tae it.
To succeed, make money first and invest it wisely.

Dinna lend yer siller as it shortens memories.
Don't lend money — people 'forget' they owe you it back.

Mony a mickle maks a muckle.
Little savings soon mount up.

Meat eaten loses the will tae pay.
People are not motivated to pay for something already used.

**Ne'er put your haun farer oot than yer sleeve
will reach.**
Spend no more than you can afford.

Some wad fley a louse for its skin.
Some folk are so mean they'd skin a flea for its skin!

Quality costs mair siller.
You only get what you pay for.

Tis folly to live poor and die rich.
Use your money and assets wisely to enjoy life.

Nae siller, nae service.
You must pay to get what you want.

Buying right is buying dear — unless fae the gerdin!
Quality is never cheap — unless it grows naturally!

He that's twa hoards will get a third.
Money creates even more money.

Don't eat the calf in the cow's wame.
Don't spend the money for bills before they are due.

Money is like the midden; it does nae guid till spread.
Money and manure are only useful when used properly.

23 OBSERVATIONS ON LIFE

A bald head is soon shaven.
Every situation has some advantage.

Follow his path and know the man.
You can only know someone by his deeds.

The plain truth is sometimes no' pretty.
The truth is not always easy to accept.

Busy tars are happy tars.
He who rows the boat doesn't have time to rock it.

Dinna mind other folk's thochts.
What other people think is not important.

We a' huv a' the time there is.
We all have the same chances.

Aw thing clangs but yer shadow.
Only your shadow has no substance.

Pleasure comes wi' enemies' woes.
We enjoy our enemies' sorrows.

Awa' an' dry yer chin.
It's time for you to be quiet.

Politicians a' hae problems wi' wind.
Politicians say little of substance.

The politicians get oor votes and siller fae the rich — I hope!
Politicians take money from the rich and votes from the poor.

The dug is mair important than the collar.
It is better to concede on unimportant issues than important ones.

Mirrors gae us what we want.
Sometimes we only see what we want to see.

He can see a midge a mile away but cannae see the wolf at his feet.
Some people are blind to problems close at hand.

A pinch o' fear an' a'body's guid.
The fear of punishment deters the wrongdoer.

Hasty was hanged, but speed-o-foot wan awa'.
Hasty actions are foolish.

Mak the best o' a bad bargain.
Console yourself by making the best of any bad situation.

The day hae e'en; the nicht hae lugs.
You cannot escape notice in this life.

Crofts and castles both get rain
Everybody has problems.

Big mouths dinna mind the task.
Nothing is impossible to those who don't have to do it
themselves.

Tradesmen aye come the half oor yer oot!
Tradesmen are always unreliable.

Throwin' dirt digs yer ain hole.
Belittling other folk will get you nowhere.

Honour and envy dinna haud hauns.
Honour and envy are incompatible.

Justice is a big virtue.
Above all, be fair.

Nae pleasure pleases some.
You can be sure if you are not pleased, you are giving
pleasure to someone else.

Ca' again — you're no a ghaist.
You're always welcome.

Pigs may whistle but they hae an ill mouth for't.
It's most unlikely!

Neglect the crofts, neglect the land.
Neglect the village and you neglect Scotland.

Aw yin spies himself first in photos.
We are all self-conscious.

It taks twa tae fecht.
Any argument has two sides to it.

As guid may haud the stirrup as he that loups on.
Everyone is equal — the groom and the horseman both.

Truth will aye stand by itsel'.
Truth will stand up to any scrutiny.

Quality and best gae oot thegither.
Quality and excellence are synonymous.

Better to say 'here it is' than 'here it was'.
Something to hand is better than something gone.

He that comes first to the hill can sit where he wants.
The earlycomer has the best choice.

Guid manners suffer bad yins.
Courtesy outshines poor manners.

Back to auld claes and purridge!
Ah, well. Back to the everyday things in life!

That's put yer gas at a peep!
That's put you in your place!

That's the ba' up on the slates noo.
Now we have a real problem!

Guid gear comes in sma' bulk.
Smaller people are just as competent as their taller
friends.

24 OLD FOLKS

Grandpas aye snore first.
The grandparent who snores is always the first to fall
asleep.

Age should bring wisdom and time to men.
A good grandpa should remember your birthday but not
your age.

Yer grandpa canny stop watchin' his work!
Your grandpa loves his work. He could watch it all day!

Crones wi' wrinkles hae nae pain.
Be thankful in old age that wrinkles don't hurt.

There's nae fools like auld fools.
The silliest fools are old ones who should know better.

**Sodger!! The only 'warhorse' he saw was in his
pipe!**
Your grandpa was never a soldier — the closest he got to
the war was smoking his Warhorse tobacco.

Auld folk are twice bairns.
Remember to care for older citizens.

Never throw yer granny aff a bus.
Don't be careless with grandmothers — they're priceless!

Dinna be auld for anither ten years.
Old age should always be ten years older than you are.

Haud yer feet, lucky dad, auld folks no fiery.
If you're getting on in age be careful, you're not so nimble.

Learnin' folks become old folks.
Great age can be achieved by continually learning
something new.

25 PATIENCE

Bide a wee.
Hold on for a bit.

The langest day will hae an end.
All things eventually come to an end.

Ane at a time is guid fishing.
Be content with your life.

Patient folk win in the end.
Patience overcomes everything.

Patience is more important than sugar!
Patience is a better virtue than flattery.

26 POSSESSIONS

Yer freen's jeelie piece always tastes better than yer ain.
People are never satisfied with what they've got.

He disnae ken the pleasures o' plenty, wha' ne'er felt the pains o' penury.
If you once had nothing then you appreciate it when you have something.

Eening orts are guid morning's fother.
Items thrown out today may be valuable in the future.

The waur o' the wear needs replacing.
Worn implements need to be replaced.

They that finds keeps; they that loses seeks.
Keeping possession is important in life.

The wife's aye welcome that comes wi' a crookit oxter.
Anyone bearing a gift is always welcome.

He that has but ane ee maun tent it weel.
Be careful with limited resources.

Mair than enough is ower much.
You can have too much of anything.

27 PRACTICAL ACTIONS

A blind man's wife needs nae painting.
Don't carry out unnecessary tasks.

A beard on a man only helps sup the oats.
Beards are only good for soaking up porridge.

We've a' got auld Scotland fur a gerdin.
Keep Scotland tidy — it's your back garden.

A short grace is guid for hungry folk.
Don't waste time; get on with the job.

Be busy like bees, naw wasps wha' get clipped.
Be a busy bee — wasps get swatted.

Daylight will keek thru a sma' hole.
You cannot cover every eventuality.

Dinna ask the Almighty — he's a busy man.
Don't pray for something you can easily do yourself.

Need makes the auld wife trot.
Necessity acts as an incentive.

Dinna care aboot nae hair — ye canny change it.
The only cure for baldness is acceptance.

Mony irons in the fire, some maun cool.
Concentrate on the main issues in life — if you take on too many some may be neglected.

Keep yer heid and feet warm and the rest will tak nae harm.
Look after the essentials._

A dug wi' twa owners is twice hungry.
Always know who is responsible for taking action.

Step ower rivers at the burn.
Address problems at their source.

Talkin' won't pay the rent.
Words don't pay bills.

Cast not oot the foul water till you bring in the clean.
Don't throw things out until the replacement has arrived.

A pun o' care winna pay an ounce o' debt.
Worrying doesn't pay the bills.

A live mouse beats a deid elephant.
Stick to live issues.

Hang a thief when he's young, and he'll no steal when he's auld.
Fix problems right away.

There is little for the rake efter the besom.
There is little need for further action after things have been accomplished.

Better be the lucky man than the lucky man's bairn.

Better go for a sure thing rather than an unlikely happening.

Don't burn down your barn to get rid o' the mice.

In life, take appropriate action — not extreme measures.

A step at a time gets you there.

Long journeys are short if divided into sections.

28 REPUTATIONS

They that get the name o' early rising may lie in bed a' day.
You can hide behind a good reputation.

A common blot is nae stain.
Don't worry about small faults which are common to everyone.

Be the thing ye would be ca'd.
To be admired you must be admirable.

Meat feeds, claith cleeds, but manners make the man.
A gentleman is known by his manners.

The bigger the cheese, the bigger the smell.
The biggest cheeses have the strongest smell!

Naething is got without pains but an ill name.
Only bad reputations are gained without effort.

Those no present are aye tae blame.
People always blame those who aren't there to defend themselves.

Guid folks mak a guid village.
It's the people, not the houses, that make the village.

He couldna punch his way oot a wet Tilly!
He's pathetic — couldn't punch his way out of a wet
newspaper!

'They' get the blame o' a'thing.
The mysterious 'they' are responsible for everything.

Credit lost is akin to broken glass.
Lost honour can never be restored.

He that blaws in the stour fills his ain e'en.
If you stir up a situation some of the fallout will settle on
you.

Better be something that naethin'.
A second-rate something is better than a first-rate nothing.

29 RESPECT

Only gae respect to the guid yins.
The good do not deserve envy.

The poor wi' courtesy are rich in life.
Poor people with manners are gentry.

The crowd's appeal make a' proud.
Public affection makes people feel special.

We're a' Jock Tamson's bairns.
We're all the same — all equal

30 SHREWDNESS

Three men can keep a secret if twa are deed.
There is no such thing as a secret.

Erring brings folks wisdom.
Every time you make a mistake, you are the wiser for it.

It's gey silly to buy frae a man pantin' in the road.
Never buy from a doubtful source.

They that see your heid see not a' your weight.
There's more to folk than meets the eye.

Choose your spouse on Saturday, but not on Sunday.
Don't choose your partner judged solely on when they're in their Sunday best.

Take a'thing bar a fist.
Refuse nothing but blows.

Ye've got it when ye can keep it.
Maturity is reached when you can keep a secret.

Be smart and shout naethin'.
Nothing is sometimes a good thing to do and always a clever thing to say.

I'm saying nowt till I see my lawyer.
I'm keeping quiet and will remain so.

A man's hat in his hands ne'er did him harm.
Humility pays.

A raggit coat is armour against the robber.
A low profile can be useful at times.

Act daft and get a free hurl.
Acting simple sometimes can get you off Scot free.

He that's deceived me once, shame fa' him.
He that's deceived me twice, shame fa' me.
Fool me once, shame on you; fool me twice, shame on me.

Ye can fool ithers but no yer auld grannie!
You cannot fool your nearest.

Gather yer thoughts before opening yer jaws.
Think before you speak.

**If ye decide to grasp the nettle make sure there's
a docken nearby.**
In any course of action, make sure there's an escape
plan.

Gae a' folk the hearin'.
Listen to folk without judgement.

Take care in love or going to court — it's tricky.
Love, honour and justice are delicate objects — handle
them with care.

Nane can play the fool sae weel as a wise man.
Appear simple — remain astute.

Bairns speak in the field what they hear by the fire.
Watch what you say in front of children.

It's no just lochs ye droon in.
Don't always assume the obvious.

A wise man has nae doctors in his will.
Be sensible in life.

A wife wha kept her supper for her breakfast, and she died 'ere day.
Use your assets wisely.

Ye're an honest man and I'm yer uncle and that's twa great lies.
Who are you kidding!

Twa thoughts, ane speech.
Think twice before you speak.

Ne'er trust muckle to an auld enemy or a new freen.
Be cautious in your dealings with old enemies and new friends.

Watch yin who always agree.
Don't trust people who always agree with the majority.

Discreet folk are better than the talkers.
The ability to be discreet is more important than the ability
to talk well.

Be canny wi' others toes when your mooth stomps aboot.
Be careful with what you say in company.

Better ken how mony beans mak five.
Look after your own interests — nobody else will!

Surprising Auld Nick's a good start.
Surprise is a good initiative to take.

He that says what he likes will hear what he disnae like.
If you're not diplomatic in your speech you may hear
unkind things about yourself.

Nae man is wise at a' times, nor wise in a' things.
Even wise people are not correct all the time.

A hungry louse bites sair.
Don't underestimate anyone.

Wisdom is best taught by distress.
Problems bring wisdom to many.

Castles fall but wise words stey.
Common sense can never be destroyed.

There are three things in a' things.
There are a number of angles to everything.

You're teachin' your granny to suck eggs.
You're telling someone something they already know all about.

He needs a lang shanket spoon that sups kail wi' the deil.
If you have business with suspicious people, be on your guard.

31 TAKING POSITIVE MEASURES

Dae weel and hae luck.
The better you prepare, the luckier you become.

**Keep busy wi' yer life and you'll no see auld
Nick approach.**
Bust out — don't rust out!

Dree oot the inch as ye hae done the span.
Get the most out of life right to the end.

Better do it than wish it.
Just wishing is no good — you need to do it!

**Wet sheep don't shrink — they shak aff the
water.**
Don't give in to misfortune.

Naebody fancies the losin'.
Nobody likes losing.

A craw is nae whiter for bein' washed.
Don't waste your time on useless tasks.

Improve yer yesterday.
Try to make today better than yesterday.

Dinna pile 'would' for the morn.
Do it today!

Dinna live yer life in a dwam.
Don't daydream.

It's guid to begin weel, but better to end weel.
Beginning something is only of value if you see it through
to the end.

He that spares to speak spares to speed.
Don't talk — act.

Men's statures gang far wi' big problems.
Difficult situations produce men of stature.

Set a stout heart to a steep hillside.
Determination will get you there.

No knowin' whit's ahead is an exciting climb.
The unexpected is often an exciting experience.

It's not the size of the dog in the fight, but the fight in the dog.
It's what's inside you that counts

Sweep auld ways fae time to time.
Tradition is a fine thing, but it needs reviewing now and then.

Hae a rich life regardless o' yer siller.
Enjoy life and don't worry about your finances.

Seek till ye find and ye'll no lose yer labour.
Don't give up until you've accomplished your task.

Even in a fallen nest ye may find a whole egg.
You can always salvage something out of disaster.

'Canna be done' means he'll do it.
If you want a Scotsman to do something, tell him it cannot be done.

The young folk dinna ken the boundaries and can do a'thing.
The young always challenge the established rules.

Convictions start small.
All our convictions were once whims.

There's as guid fish in the sea as ever cam oot it.
There are plenty of opportunities still to be had.

Strength o' mind defeats a'thing.
Willpower overcomes all situations.

Pit mair in than ye tak oot.
Successful people put more into life than they take out.

Fools and bairns should no see half done work.
Be an example, especially to those who need it.

Don't make a right souch about naething.
Don't make a fuss over nothing.

Ambition's a great seed.
Nothing can stop ambition from growing.

Getting up's mair important than fallin' doon.
The achievement is not in never falling but in rising after every slip.

In life, you should try to set the heather on fire.
In life you should always try to do really well.

32 TIME

Yer only here a wee while — so be nice.
Be quick to be kind — life is short.

Your time is yours, dinna let ithers spend it.
Time is the coinage of life; don't let other people waste it
for you.

Better late here than early wi' the angels.
Slow down — better ten minutes late in this world than
twenty years early for the next.

Late in the morn — late a' day.
If you rise late you run late all day.

The snug five minutes afore ye rise is precious.
The five minutes in bed before you rise is quality time.

**A day to come seems langer than a year that's
gone.**
The final minute always seems the longest.

If ye dinna feed the cat ye'll feed the mice.
Do it now or the situation will get worse.

33 WEATHER

The rain is God's way o' cleanin' the coos!
Even bad weather has its uses.

Cast not a clout till May be oot.
Don't assume it's summer until the May blossom comes.

Yer grandpa's like the weather — nae pattern.
The Scottish climate is like your grandfather —
unpredictable.

January's cauld can be used.
Even January can be a lovely month if you know what to
do with it.

Stormy weather promises dinna last.
Promises made during tough times don't always last.

34 WORK

Nae mair work, nae mair holidays.
The problem with retirement is you cannot take a day off!

He that wad thrive must rise by five; he that has thriven may lie till seven.
Only if you've already made it in life, can you stay in bed.

Dae mair than just dream aboot it.
If you want anything, work for it — don't just dream about it.

Nae sweat, nae sweet.
Good things only come from hard work.

Aw life's purpose is doin'.
The purpose of life is life with a purpose.

There's mair to ploughing than whistling.
Many an apparently simple task requires considerable expertise.

Skill and love gae best.
When skill and love work together the result is perfection.

The stout horse aye gets the hard work.
The willing get the hard work to do.

GLOSSARY

ane	one	maun	must
aye	always	midden	dunghill
bairn	a child	mither	mother
baith	both	minent	a minute
besom	a broom	mony	many
brae	hillside	moose	mouse
breeks	trousers	muckle	large
burn	stream	nae	no
canna	cannot	ne'er	never
cauld	cold	oor	our
causey	street	oot	out
deid	dead	ower	over
deil	devil	oxter	armpit
dinna	don't	piece	sandwich
draff	spent grain	raggit	ragged
dwam	stupor	reels	dances
e'e/e'en	eye/eyes	sair	sore
e'en	even	scabbit	ill-looking
farer	further	sindle	seldom
fash	trouble/upset	smit	infect
faur	far	souch	fuss
fother	fodder	stour	dirt, dust
freen	a friend	sugh	a ditch
gae, gaes	give, gives	tae	to
gang	go	tak	take
gat	got	tars	sailors
ghaist	ghost	thocht	a thought
guid	good	thon	yonder
hame	home	thran	train or shape
haud	hold	unco	uncommon
hoos	house	wame	stomach
kail	broth	wan	one
kame	comb	waur	worse
keek	glance	waur	to spend money
kin	relations	wean	child
laldie	punishment	ween	to boast
lang	long	weird	destiny
louse	flea	woodie	piece of wood
lum	chimney	wrang	wrong
maist	most	wylie-coat	flannel coat